ACE

Group Fitness Instructor

Master the Manual

A Study Guide to Accompany the
ACE Group Fitness Instructor Manual
Second Edition

AMERICAN COUNCIL ON EXERCISE

4851 Paramount Drive, San Diego, California 92123, 800-825-3636, www.acefitness.org

Second edition

Copyright © 2007 American Council on Exercise®

Printed in the United States of America.

ISBN 10: 1-890720-21-6
ISBN 13: 978-1-890720-21-6

A B C D E

Distributed by:
American Council on Exercise
P.O. Box 910449
San Diego, CA 92191-0449
(858) 279-8227
(858) 279-8064 (FAX)
www.ACEfitness.org

Author: Richard J. Seibert, M.A., M.Ed.

Editors: Daniel J. Green & Christine J. Ekeroth
Technical Editor: Cedric X. Bryant, Ph.D.
Design: Karen McGuire
Production: Sandra Pennock
Associate Editor: Marion Webb
Technical Consultant: Christine "CC" Cunningham, M.S.

Table of Contents

How to Use This Study Guide

Welcome to *Master the Manual,* a study guide designed as a companion to the *ACE Group Fitness Instructor Manual,* Second Edition. The exercises in this book are designed to help you master the basic concepts of group exercise instruction by breaking them into manageable concepts that you can apply to real-life situations.

Each chapter of the study guide is divided into sections. **Getting Started** introduces you to the material by providing objectives and vocabulary words to concentrate on as you read the corresponding chapter in the manual. **Expand Your Knowledge** will test your comprehension through a variety of exercises and drills. **Show What You Know** exercises your ability to apply what you have learned to real-life situations. Some chapters will take you one step further, providing activities to expand your skills in **Practice What You Know.** If you are using the *ACE Group Fitness Instructor Manual* in conjunction with this study guide to prepare for the ACE Group Fitness Instructor Certification Examination, you should focus not only on learning the concepts, but also on applying them to group fitness situations. This application of knowledge will best assist you in both teaching group exercise and preparing for the examination. Follow these steps to get the most from *Master the Manual.*

Step One: Read

Read the student objectives for each chapter, and then read the corresponding chapter in the *ACE Group Fitness Instructor Manual.* Read one chapter at a time rather than attempting to read the entire manual at one sitting. As you read, look for the vocabulary works listed at the beginning of each study guide chapter. When you come across one, mark it in your text.

Step Two: Define

After you have read each chapter and marked the vocabulary words, define each on a separate piece of paper. Write the definition even if you feel you already know it. Learning is a sensory experience, so the more senses you can involve in the learning process the more you will be able to retain. Writing down definitions, or putting your thoughts into words, will help you to remember the material more clearly.

Step Three: Exercises

After defining the vocabulary words, skim through the chapter in the manual again. Attempt to do the exercises in the study guide without looking at the manual. Check your answers against the key that appears in Appendix B, which begins on page 86. If you answer a question incorrectly, go back to the text and find out why your answer is wrong. Make a note to yourself for future reference. If you correctly answered a question, but feel you were guessing, go back to the manual and read that section again. Do not assume you will remember it.

Step Four: Final Notes

Now is the time to go back to the objectives on the first page of each study guide chapter. Mark any areas you are unsure of or want to learn more about, and reread the related sections in the manual. Use the references and suggested reading lists at the end of each manual chapter to find sources for more information.

The focus of this workbook is on learning and retention. That is why we do not grade the exercises or relate the results to either a score or to your chance for success on the ACE exam. No textbook or study guide can predict your performance on a certification examination. If you feel you need additional preparation, call ACE to receive information on ACE exam preparation materials and training programs.

1 *Exercise Physiology*

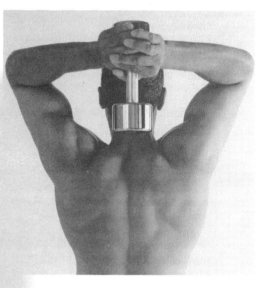

Vocabulary

- ▼ physical fitness
- ▼ range of motion (ROM)
- ▼ lean body mass
- ▼ body fat
- ▼ adenosine triphosphate (ATP)
- ▼ adenosine diphosphate (ADP)
- ▼ creatine phosphate (CP)
- ▼ glycolysis
- ▼ lactic acid
- ▼ lactate
- ▼ mitochondria
- ▼ exercise specificity
- ▼ central nervous system (CNS)
- ▼ motor unit
- ▼ sliding filament theory
- ▼ Valsalva maneuver
- ▼ hypertrophy
- ▼ reversibility principle
- ▼ atrophy
- ▼ delayed onset muscle soreness (DOMS)
- ▼ stretch reflexes
- ▼ muscle spindle
- ▼ Golgi tendon organ
- ▼ hemoglobin
- ▼ heart rate
- ▼ stroke volume
- ▼ cardiac output
- ▼ steady state
- ▼ anaerobic threshold (AT)
- ▼ overload

Getting Started

This chapter describes how the body functions during physical activity. Applying the foundations of exercise physiology is essential to safe and effective exercise programs. After completing this section you will have a **better understanding of:**

- ◆ the five components of physical fitness
- ◆ the bioenergetics of exercise
- ◆ the three energy pathway systems
- ◆ basic organization of the nervous system
- ◆ basic organization of the muscular system
- ◆ the cardiovascular and respiratory systems
- ◆ the acute effects of exercise
- ◆ the long-term effects of training
- ◆ environmental considerations when exercising

Reading Assignment

Read Chapter 1 of the *ACE Group Fitness Instructor Manual*, paying special attention to the words listed in the box to the left. After you have read the chapter, define these words on a separate piece of paper.

Expand Your Knowledge

I. Match the components of physical fitness on the right to the definitions on the left.

a. _____ the capacity of the heart, blood vessels, and lungs to deliver oxygen and nutrients to the working muscles and tissues during sustained exercise and to remove the metabolic waste products that would result in fatigue

b. _____ the ability to move joints through their normal full range of motion (ROM)

c. _____ the ability of a muscle or muscle group to exert force against a resistance over a sustained period of time

d. _____ the makeup of the body, considering fat weight and fat-free weight

e. _____ the maximal force a muscle or muscle group can exert during a single contraction

1. body composition

2. muscular endurance

3. muscular strength

4. cardiovascular endurance

5. flexibility

II. Fill in the space to the right of each letter by placing an (F) if it is a product or result of fat metabolism, a (C) if it is a product or result of carbohydrate metabolism, and (P) if it is a product or result of protein metabolism. In some cases, more than one response may be appropriate.

a. _____ glycogen

b. _____ ATP

c. _____ lean body mass

d. _____ adipose tissue

e. _____ amino acids

f. _____ glucose

III. Describe the major differences between the following pairs of words or phrases.

a. anaerobic glycolysis and aerobic glycolysis

_____

_____

b. concentric contraction and eccentric contraction

_____

_____

c. static stretching and ballistic stretching

_____

_____

d. systolic blood pressure and diastolic blood pressure

_____

_____

e. exercise for type 1 diabetes and exercise for type 2 diabetes

_____

_____

f. vasoconstriction and vasodilation

_____

_____

g. sensory neurons and motor neurons

_____

_____

IV. List the five tips for
exercising in the heat.

1. _____

_____

2. _____

_____

3. _____

_____

4. _____

_____

5. _____

_____

V. Determine whether the
following characteristics
are examples of fast-twitch
(FT) or slow-twitch (ST)
muscle fibers.

a. _____ high capacity for anaerobic glycolysis

b. _____ most responsive to endurance activities

c. _____ well equipped for oxygen delivery

d. _____ utilized for rapid, powerful movements

e. _____ have a large number of mitochondria

VI. List the four tips for exercising in the cold.

1. _____

_____

2. _____

_____

3. _____

_____

4. _____

_____

VII. Determine whether the following conditions are examples of oxygen deficit (DEF), steady state (SS), or excess postexercise oxygen consumption (EPOC).

a. _____ a temporarily elevated oxygen consumption as the body returns to resting levels

b. _____ the first two to four minutes of exercise

c. _____ homeostatic conditions are restored

d. _____ oxygen supply equals oxygen demand

e. _____ oxygen supply is less than oxygen demand

VIII. Place the following steps in oxygen utilization in the proper order.

a. _____ oxygen enters the muscle fibers

b. _____ oxygen enters Kreb Cycle

c. _____ oxygen diffuses through the pulmonary membranes

d. _____ oxygen enters mitochondria

e. _____ oxygen enters heart

f. _____ oxygen enters lungs

g. _____ oxygen enters blood stream

h. _____ oxygen binds with hemoglobin

IX. Write the formula for each of the following terms.

a. cardiac output: _____

_____

b. resynthesis of ATP by CP: _____

_____

c. anaerobic glycolysis: _____

_____

X. *List and describe the three guidelines for improving cardiovascular-respiratory endurance.*

1. _____
_____

2. _____
_____

3. _____
_____

XI. *Describe the relationship between the following pairs of words or phrases.*

a. myosin and actin _____
_____
_____

b. anaerobic threshold and lactic acid _____
_____
_____

c. warm-up and stretching _____
_____
_____

d. stretching and delayed onset muscle soreness (DOMS) _____
_____
_____

Show What You Know

I. You are an instructor at a resort on top of a scenic 12,000-foot (3658-meter) mountain. List some of the potential problems visiting exercise participants might face in this high-altitude environment and what precautions you may take to avoid them.

_____

_____

_____

_____

_____

_____

_____

_____

II. Calculate cardiac output max given the following information:
Max SV: 125 mL/beat
Max HR: 200 beats/min

_____

_____

_____

_____

_____

_____

Practice What You Know

Calculate the average time you spend on each of the five components of physical fitness each week.

2 Fundamentals of Anatomy

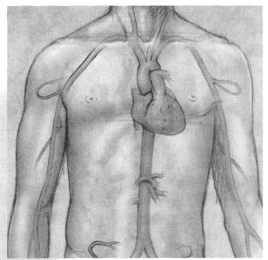

Vocabulary

- ▼ arterioles
- ▼ capillaries
- ▼ distal
- ▼ venules
- ▼ cartilage
- ▼ primary bronchi
- ▼ bronchioles
- ▼ alveoli
- ▼ bronchial tree
- ▼ receptors
- ▼ proprioceptors
- ▼ kinesthetic awareness
- ▼ stretch reflex
- ▼ levers
- ▼ diaphysis
- ▼ epiphyses
- ▼ connective tissue
- ▼ collagen
- ▼ Wolff's Law
- ▼ amenorrhea
- ▼ articulation
- ▼ force
- ▼ isometric
- ▼ agonist
- ▼ antagonist
- ▼ synergists

Getting Started

This chapter describes the structure and function of the five major systems within the human body: the cardiovascular system, the respiratory system, the nervous system, the skeletal system, and the muscular system. After completing this section you will have a better understanding of:

- ◆ basic anatomical terms
- ◆ the functional anatomy of the heart
- ◆ external, internal, and cellular respiration
- ◆ the central and peripheral nervous systems
- ◆ the axial and appendicular skeleton
- ◆ the structure and type of movement allowed by joints
- ◆ muscles of the lower and upper extremity

Reading Assignment

Read Chapter 2 of the *ACE Group Fitness Instructor Manual*, paying special attention to the words listed in the box to the left. After you have read the chapter, define these words on a separate piece of paper.

Expand Your Knowledge

I. Match the anatomical, directional, and regional terms on the right to their descriptions on the left.

a. _____ toward the attached end of the limb, origin of the structure, or midline of the body

b. _____ the sole or bottom of the foot

c. _____ away from the head

d. _____ a longitudinal (imaginary) line that divides the body into anterior and posterior halves

e. _____ regional term referring to the low back; the portion between the abdomen and the pelvis

f. _____ toward the back

g. _____ toward the midline of the body

h. _____ a longitudinal (imaginary) line that divides the body or any of its parts into right and left halves

1. proximal

2. posterior

3. plantar

4. inferior

5. medial

6. sagittal plane

7. frontal plane

8. lumbar

II. Describe the major differences between the following pairs of words or phrases.

a. arteries and veins _____

_____

b. axial skeleton and appendicular skeleton _____

_____

c. periosteum and endosteum _____

_____

d. oxygen and carbon dioxide _____

_____

e. the stretch reflex and the GTO reflex _____

_____

*III. Label the following diagram of the heart, placing the name of the structure to the **RIGHT** of the letter. Place a number to the **LEFT** of the letter to indicate chronological order of blood flow beginning with blood entering through the superior and inferior vena cava.*

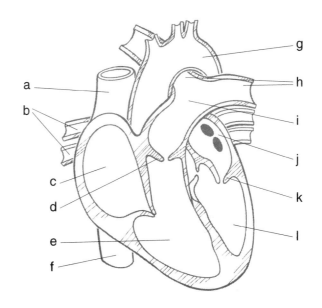

___ a _____   ___ g _____

___ b _____   ___ h _____

___ c _____   ___ i _____

___ d _____   ___ j _____

___ e _____   ___ k _____

___ f _____   ___ l _____

IV. List the artery or vein that carries blood to and from the following sites.

a. to the kidneys from the abdominal aorta _____

b. from the dural sinuses to the subclavian vein _____

c. to the deep palmar arch from the brachial artery _____

d. from the lungs to the heart _____

e. to the thoracic aorta from the ascending aorta _____

V. Determine whether the following describes external respiration (E), internal respiration (I), or cellular respiration (C).

a. _____ the utilization of oxygen in energy production

b. _____ the release of carbon dioxide into the atmosphere

c. _____ carbon dioxide production

d. _____ carbon dioxide uptake by the blood

e. _____ oxygen uptake by the blood

f. _____ oxygen release by the blood

VI. For the following nerve roots, name the plexus area and describe what it innervates.

a. C1 through C4 _____

_____

_____

b. C5 through T1 _____

_____

_____

c. T1 through L4 _____

_____

_____

d. L4 through S4 _____

_____

_____

VII. List the five functions of the skeletal system.

1. _____

_____

_____

2. _____

_____

_____

3. _____

_____

_____

4. _____

_____

_____

5. _____

_____

_____

VIII. Determine whether the following joints are synovial (S), cartilaginous (C), or fibrous (F).

a. _____ radioulnar

b. _____ intervertebral disks

c. _____ ribs and the sternum

d. _____ hip joint

e. _____ thumb

f. _____ distal tibia and fibula

g. _____ wrist

IX. *Describe the major characteristics of the following bone classifications.*

a. long _____

_____

b. short _____

_____

c. flat _____

_____

d. irregular _____

_____

X. *Match the human movement terminology on the left to its definition on the right (from anatomical position). Indicate to the far left if the movement occurs in the sagittal (S), frontal (F), or transverse (T) plane, or if it is multiplanar (M).*

Plane   Match

a. _____ _____ flexion

b. _____ _____ abduction

c. _____ _____ internal rotation

d. _____ _____ pronation

e. _____ _____ elevation

f. _____ _____ extension

g. _____ _____ eversion

h. _____ _____ adduction

1. rotating the hand and wrist from the elbow to the palm down position (elbow flexed)

2. rotation of the foot to direct the plantar surface outward

3. bringing the legs and arms toward the midline of the body during a jumping jack

4. turning the right leg along the axis of the femur toward the left leg

5. lifting the arms to the side during a lateral dumbbell raise

6. lifting the lower arms during a front biceps curl at the elbow joint

7. shrugging the shoulders as you say "I don't know"

8. lowering the lower arms at the elbow joint during a front biceps curl

XI. Identify the muscles on the following illustrations as indicated.

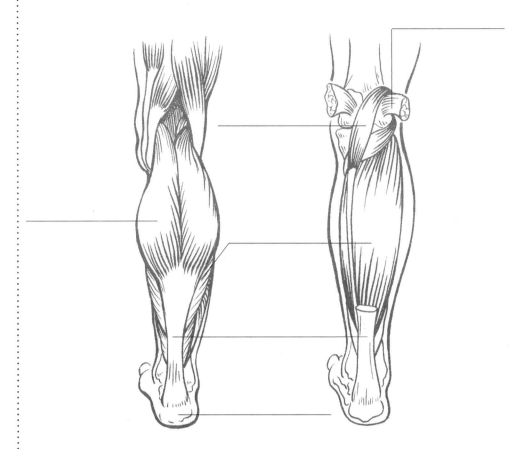

Identify the muscles on the following illustrations as indicated.

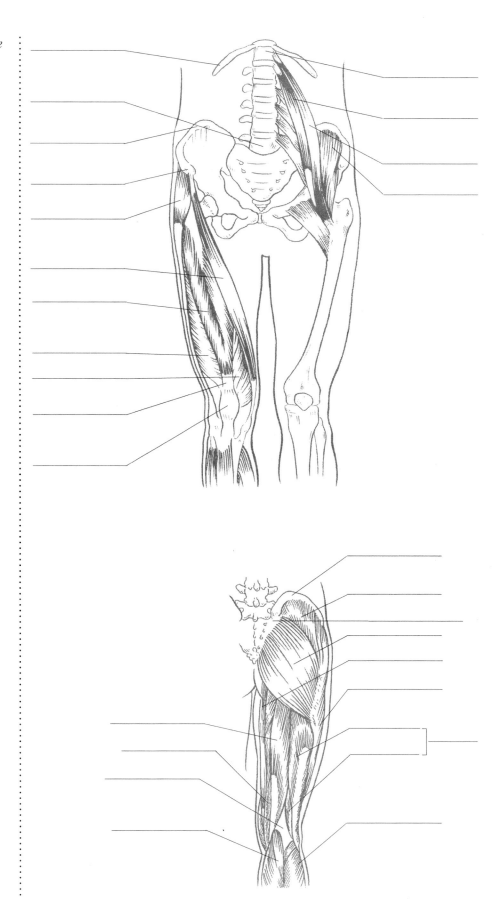

Identify the muscles on the following illustrations as indicated.

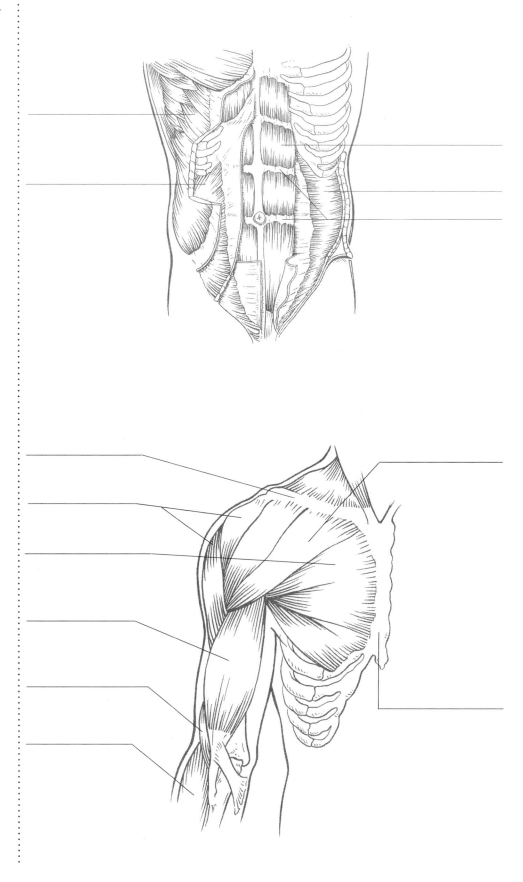

Identify the muscles on the following illustrations as indicated.

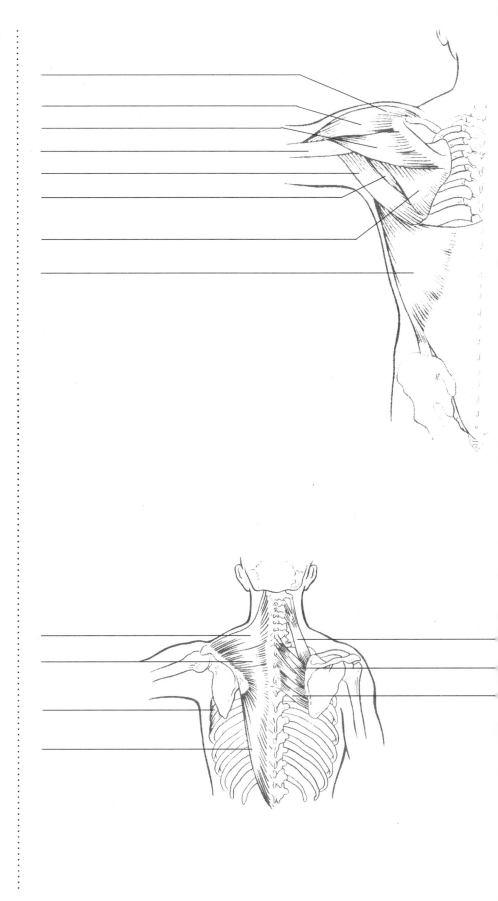

XII. Name the primary muscles or muscle groups that are used during the following movements.

a. extension at the elbow _____

_____

b. elevation of the scapula _____

_____

c. dorsiflexion at the ankle _____

_____

d. abduction at the hip _____

_____

e. compression of the abdomen _____

_____

f. extension of the trunk _____

_____

3 *Fundamentals of Applied Kinesiology*

Vocabulary

- ▾ kinesiology
- ▾ law of inertia
- ▾ law of acceleration
- ▾ law of reaction
- ▾ applied force
- ▾ hyperextension
- ▾ prime movers
- ▾ dorsiflexion
- ▾ plantarflexion
- ▾ neutral spine position
- ▾ lordosis
- ▾ kyphosis
- ▾ scoliosis
- ▾ shoulder joint complex
- ▾ scapulothoracic articulation
- ▾ scapulohumeral rhythm

Getting Started

This chapter describes the fundamentals of how the human body performs movement. Understanding this information is the first step in designing exercise classes that are safe and effective for your participants. After completing this section you will have a better understanding of:

- ◆ the science of kinesiology
- ◆ the laws of inertia, acceleration, and reaction
- ◆ the kinesiology of the lower extremity
- ◆ how the spine and pelvis create movement
- ◆ the kinesiology of the upper extremity

Reading Assignment

Read Chapter 3 of the *ACE Group Fitness Instructor Manual*, paying special attention to the words listed in the box to the left. After you have read the chapter, define these words on a separate piece of paper.

Expand Your Knowledge

*I. Explain the acronym SITS
and list its components.*

SITS = _____

_____

S = _____

I = _____

T = _____

S = _____

*II. Indicate the natural law
best described by each of the
following examples.*

a. Momentum increases as mass increases if velocity is held constant (M = mv).

_____

_____

b. Lifting 150 pounds (67.5 kg) is more difficult than lifting 50 pounds (22.5 kg).

_____

_____

c. Impact forces are greater from a 10-inch step than an 8-inch step.

_____

_____

III. List the four segments that make up the shoulder joint complex.

1. _____

2. _____

3. _____

4. _____

IV. List the primary movers for each of the following movements.

a. hip extension _____

_____

b. knee extension _____

_____

c. plantarflexion _____

_____

d. hip abduction _____

_____

V. Describe the major differences between the following pairs of words or phrases.

a. lordosis and kyphosis _____

_____

b. external oblique and internal oblique _____

_____

c. retraction and protraction _____

_____

d. concentric contraction of the upper trapezius and lower trapezius _____

_____

VI. List the three components of muscular balance.

1. _____

   _____

2. _____

   _____

3. _____

   _____

VII. List the major muscles for the following areas.

a. posterior shoulder girdle _____

_____

b. glenohumeral joint _____

_____

c. anterior shoulder girdle _____

_____

VIII. Match the muscle on the right to the description on the left.

a. _____ when stimulated unilaterally, lateral flexion to that same side occurs

b. _____ it extends and horizontally rotates the arm at the shoulder

c. _____ the only muscle of the quadriceps femoris that crosses the hip joint

d. _____ a very large muscle that comprises the bulk of the muscle on the anterior chest wall

e. _____ to stretch this muscle, stand in a forward lunge position with one knee flexed and foot flat, and the heel of the other leg off the floor

f. _____ nicknamed "little lat"

1. pectoralis major

2. posterior deltoid

3. iliocostalis, longissimus, and spinalis

4. iliopsoas

5. teres major

6. rectus femoris

a. standing squats with dumbbells to 135 degrees _____

_____

_____

_____

_____

b. participant with lordosis _____

_____

_____

_____

_____

c. seated military press with the bar behind the neck _____

_____

_____

_____

_____

d. standing straight-leg abduction to target the gluteus maximus

_____

_____

_____

_____

CHAPTER 4

Introduction to Nutrition

Vocabulary

- ▼ nutrition
- ▼ kilocalories
- ▼ calories
- ▼ total energy expenditure
- ▼ basal metabolic rate (BMR)
- ▼ triglycerides
- ▼ macronutrients
- ▼ monosaccharides
- ▼ disaccharides
- ▼ glycemic index
- ▼ fiber
- ▼ vitamins
- ▼ minerals
- ▼ hydrogenation
- ▼ recommended daily allowances (RDA)
- ▼ trace minerals
- ▼ dehydration
- ▼ dietary fiber
- ▼ antioxidants
- ▼ energy deficit
- ▼ ergogenic aid
- ▼ eating disorders
- ▼ hyponatremia

Getting Started

This chapter provides information on the basics of nutrition for physically active adults as well as putting together a healthy diet. After completing this section you will have a better understanding of:

- ◆ the four basic sets of dietary guidelines
- ◆ the human body and its energy systems
- ◆ the four classes of nutrients
- ◆ how to guide your participants in making healthy food choices
- ◆ the relationship between nutrition and disease
- ◆ ergogenic aids
- ◆ eating disorders

Reading Assignment

Read Chapter 4 of the *ACE Group Fitness Instructor Manual*, paying special attention to the words listed in the box to the left. After you have read the chapter, define these words on a separate piece of paper.

Expand Your Knowledge

I. Fill in the space to the left of each letter by placing a (C) if it describes the carbohydrate food class, an (F) if it describes the fat food class, and a (P) if it describes the protein food class. In some cases, more than one response may be appropriate.

a. _____ 4 kcal/g energy content

b. _____ poultry, dairy, red meats, and tofu

c. _____ whole grain, breads, legumes, and vegetables

d. _____ 9 kcal/g energy content

e. _____ olive oil, avocado, butter, and hydrogenated vegetable shortening

II. Describe the major differences between the following pairs of words or phrases.

a. viscous fibers and incompletely fermented fibers _____

_____

_____

b. simple carbohydrates and complex carbohydrates_____

_____

_____

c. essential and nonessential amino acids_____

_____

_____

d. low-density lipoproteins (LDL) and high-density lipoproteins (HDL)_____

_____

_____

e. saturated fats and unsaturated fats_____

_____

_____

III. List five tips for increasing dietary fiber.

1. _____

_____

2. _____

_____

3. _____

_____

4. _____

_____

5. _____

_____

IV. List the recommended intake and the primary functions of the following nutrients.

a. carbohydrate _____

_____

b. protein _____

_____

c. fat _____

_____

d. water _____

_____

e. fiber _____

_____

f. cholesterol _____

_____

V. Fill in the space to the right of each letter by writing (AN) if it describes anorexia nervosa, (BN) if it describes bulimia nervosa, and (BED) if it describes binge eating disorder. In some cases, more than one response may be appropriate.

a. _____ consuming huge amounts of food prior to purging

b. _____ denial of both hunger and thinness

c. _____ obsession with thinness

d. _____ consuming huge amounts of food without purging

e. _____ overwhelming feelings of guilt and emotional trauma

VI. Describe the relationship between the following pairs of words or phrases.

a. cardiovascular disease (CVD) and fat _____

_____

_____

b. a high intake of sodium and high blood pressure _____

_____

_____

c. protein powders and body builders _____

_____

_____

d. caffeine and exercise _____

_____

_____

e. phytochemicals and cancer _____

_____

_____

VII. Fill in the blanks.

a. It is estimated that with weight loss, _____ % of people with hypertension will have lower blood pressures.

b. The fat-soluble vitamins are _____.

c. The water-soluble vitamins are _____.

d. Pregnant women should consume _____ grams of carbohydrate one hour prior to exercise.

Show What You Know

I. Calculate resting energy
expenditure for an
individual who weighs
132 pounds (59.5 kg).

_____

_____

_____

II. Identify the nutritional
deficiency/problem and
create healthy diet recommendations given the
case study provided
on the right.

Case Study: A 45-year-old female participant is not consuming milk or dairy because she is lactose intolerant.

Deficiency/Problem: _____

Recommendations: _____

_____

_____

_____

_____

_____

_____

_____

_____

_____

III. An exercise participant wants to lose 10 pounds (4.5 kg) by increasing his energy expenditure. He wants to add 500 kcal worth of exercise every other day (7x/2 weeks). How many kcal will he have to burn and how long will it take him to lose 10 pounds (4.5 kg)?

_____

_____

_____

_____

_____

_____

_____

Practice What You Know

I. Inquire about your state's licensure laws governing the practice of nutrition in your state or local government.

II. Track your daily food intake for one week. Compare your food intake to the MyPyramid Food Guidance System.

5 *Health Screening*

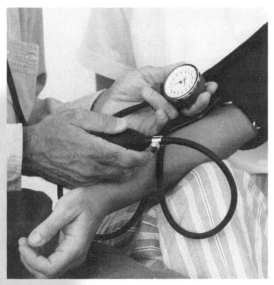

Vocabulary

- ▼ congenital
- ▼ hypertrophic cardiomyopathy
- ▼ health screening
- ▼ risk factor
- ▼ cardiovascular disease
- ▼ graded exercise test
- ▼ Physical Activity Readiness Questionnaire (PAR-Q)
- ▼ risk stratification
- ▼ echocardiography
- ▼ preparticipation screening

Getting Started

This chapter focuses on procedures group fitness instructors can implement to help protect participants when initiating exercise or athletic programs. After completing this section you will have a better understanding of:

- ◆ pre-exercise health-risk appraisal
- ◆ disease risk stratification
- ◆ the Physical Activity Readiness Questionnaire (PAR-Q)
- ◆ selecting appropriate medical/physical examinations
- ◆ current issues regarding the cardiovascular screening of athletes
- ◆ the effects of medications on heart-rate (HR) response

Reading Assignment

Read Chapter 5 of the *ACE Group Fitness Instructor Manual,* paying special attention to the words listed in the box to the left. After you have read the chapter, define these words on a separate piece of paper.

Expand Your Knowledge

I. Describe the function of the health-screening steps on the right.

a. health appraisal questionnaire_____

_____

_____

b. stratification according to disease risk _____

_____

_____

c. referral to a healthcare provider for medical evaluation_____

_____

_____

II. In the space provided, place an (L) if the participant is at Low Risk, place an (M) if the participant is at Moderate Risk, or place an (H) if the participant is at High Risk.

1. _____ 32-year-old female with no known diseases or risk factors

2. _____ 50-year-old female with 35% body fat and type 2 diabetes

3. _____ 28-year-old female with a presence of known, stable cardiovascular disease

4. _____ 52-year-old male, more than 25 pounds (11 kg) overweight, with blood pressure controlled with medication

5. _____ 42-year-old male with mild hypertension

III. Fill in the blanks.

a. For most people, regular exercise reduces the risk of heart disease by about _____ as compared to those who are physically inactive.

b. Approximately _____ of Americans suffer heart attacks during or after exercise each year.

c. For patients with heart disease, the incidence of a heart attack or death during exercise is _____ times that of otherwise healthy individuals.

d. More than _____ of all Americans have some form of cardiovascular disease by age 55, and prevalence rises with age.

IV. List the five characteristics that describe persons who tend to suffer heart attacks during or after exercise.

1. _____

_____

2. _____

_____

3. _____

_____

4. _____

_____

5. _____

_____

V. *Fill in the chart to the right by placing a (↑) if the medication causes an increase, a (↓) if the medication causes a decrease, and a (←→) if the medication causes an insignificant effect in individuals without angina. In some cases, more than one response may be appropriate.*

Medications	Resting HR	Exercising HR	Exercise Performance
Antihistamines			
Antihypertensives			
Beta-adrenergic blocking agents			
Caffeine			
Calcium channel blockers			
Diuretics			

VI. *Fill in the space to the right of each letter by placing an (ME) if the person requires a medical examination, an (ET) if the person requires an exercise test and (NR) if neither is required. In some cases, no more than one response may be appropriate.*

a. _____ healthy 50-year-old male who is inactive, beginning a moderate exercise program

b. _____ healthy 25-year-old, beginning vigorous exercise

c. _____ healthy 49-year-old man, beginning a vigorous exercise program

d. _____ 51-year-old female with presence of known, stable cardiovascular disease, beginning a moderate exercise program

e. _____ 39-year-old sedentary female with type 2 diabetes complications during exercise, beginning moderate exercise

VII. *Describe the relationship between the following pairs of words or phrases.*

a. cardiovascular screening and competitive athletes_____

_____

_____

b. health/fitness facilities and older participants _____

_____

_____

c. health screening and physician referral form _____

_____

_____

Show What You Know

I. An exercise participant, Kara Lott, is excited about starting an exercise program. Kara answers "yes" to question #6 on the Physical Activity Readiness Questionnaire (PAR-Q) and explains that she is taking beta-adrenergic channel blockers to keep her blood pressure under control.

a. What is the next step? _____

_____

_____

_____

_____

b. How will her blood pressure medication affect her exercising heart rate?

_____

_____

_____

_____

_____

II. An exercise participant, Everett Reddie, is celebrating his 46th birthday. Everett likes to exercise at 15 or 16 on the 6 to 20 ratings of perceived exertion (RPE) scale and is healthy. What modifications will you need to make for Everett now that he is 46 years old?

_____

_____

_____

_____

_____

_____

Practice What You Know

I. Use the forms from the **ACE Group Fitness Instructor Manual** *to perform a pre-exercise health appraisal. Ask a friend or relative to act as an exercise participant for a practice session.*

II. Create a list of three qualified physicians that can be used in case participants ask you for the name of a physician.

6

CHAPTER

6 *Group Exercise Program Design*

Vocabulary

- ▼ field tests
- ▼ hydrostatic weighing
- ▼ bioelectrical impedance
- ▼ near-infrared (NIR) light interactance
- ▼ anthropometric assessments
- ▼ oxygen uptake
- ▼ step tests
- ▼ body mass index
- ▼ electrocardiogram
- ▼ talk test
- ▼ maximal HR formula
- ▼ target heart rate
- ▼ resting heart rate
- ▼ maximal heart rate

Getting Started

This chapter describes the principles needed when designing the following segments of a group exercise class: pre-class preparation, warm-up, cardiorespiratory, muscular strength and endurance, and flexibility. After completing this section you will have a better understanding of:

- ◆ characteristics of a group fitness instructor
- ◆ creating a healthy emotional class environment
- ◆ applicable field tests and protocols
- ◆ methods for offering options
- ◆ how to prepare for a group exercise class
- ◆ components of a warm-up
- ◆ guidelines for the cardiorespiratory segment
- ◆ guidelines for the muscular strength and endurance segment
- ◆ guidelines for the flexibility segment

Reading Assignment

Read Chapter 6 of the *ACE Group Fitness Instructor Manual,* paying special attention to the words listed in the box to the left. After you have read the chapter, define these words on a separate piece of paper.

Expand Your Knowledge

I. Describe the overall goal for each of the following components of a group exercise class.

a. pre-class preparation _____

_____

_____

b. warm-up segment _____

_____

_____

c. cardiorespiratory segment _____

_____

_____

d. muscular strength and endurance segment _____

_____

_____

e. flexibility segment _____

_____

_____

II. Describe the major differences between the following pairs of words or phrases.

a. student-centered instructor and teacher-centered instructor _____

_____

_____

b. hydrostatic weighing and anthropometric assessments_____

_____

_____

c. maximal heart-rate formula (HRmax) and percent of heart-rate reserve

(Karvonen formula)_____

_____

_____   _____

d. high waist-to-hip ratio and low waist-to-hip ratio _____

_____

_____

III. List the muscles that should be stretched for the following categories.

a. muscles used in daily activity _____

_____

b. indoor cycling class _____

_____

c. kickboxing class _____

_____

IV. List the 2006 ACSM recommendations for fitness for healthy adults.

a. Frequency _____

_____

b. Intensity _____

_____

c. Duration _____

_____

d. Mode _____

_____

e. Resistance training _____

_____

f. Flexibility _____

_____

V. Describe the method for taking heart rates at the following pulse sites.

a. radial _____

_____

b. carotid _____

_____

c. temporal _____

_____

VI. Using heart-rate reserve (Karvonen's formula) calculate the target heart-rate range for a 45-year-old female with a resting heart rate of 65.

a. predicted maximum heart rate _____

b. heart-rate reserve _____

c. 85% _____

d. 50% _____

VII. Fill in the space to the right of each letter by placing an (S) if it describes a student-centered instructor or a (T) if it describes a teacher-centered instructor.

a. _____ Good job!

b. _____ Your heart rate will recover faster over time.

c. _____ If I do it, you have to do it!

d. _____ Watch your alignment in the mirror.

e. _____ I'm the only one looking after you.

f. _____ C'mon now, you want to look good this weekend, don't you?

VIII. List the three major reasons for gradually increasing intensity.

1. _____
   _____

2. _____
   _____

3. _____
   _____

IX. What are the positive and negative aspects of including stretches in the warm-up?

a. positive aspects _____
   _____

b. negative aspects _____
   _____

X. List the four methods for monitoring exercise intensity.

1. _____
   _____

2. _____
   _____

3. _____
   _____

4. _____
   _____

Show What You Know

I. What is the classification or category based on the following fitness assessment results?

Bob Smith
Age: 39 years old
Body fat: 15%
$\dot{V}O_2max$:
    41 (mL/kg/min)
Waist: 34 inches (86 cm)
Hip: 33 inches (84 cm)
Push-ups: 32
Trunk flexibility:
    9 inches (23 cm)

a. $\dot{V}O_2max$ _____

_____

b. body fat _____

_____

c. waist-to-hip ratio _____

_____

d. push-ups _____

_____

e. trunk flexibility _____

_____

II. An exercise participant, Rosie Cheaks, has been working hard to lose weight. Her weight is 165 pounds (74 kg) and her height is 5 feet 6 inches (168 cm). Calculate her BMI and determine her weight category.

a. BMI = _____

_____

_____

_____

b. Category = _____

_____

Practice What You Know

I. Using HR reserve (Karvonen's formula), determine your target HR range.

a. predicted maximum heart rate = _____

b. heart-rate range = _____

c. Upper (85%) = _____

d. Lower (50%) = _____

II. Identify the items listed in the Class Format Summary Checklist on pages 193–194 by observing three different types of classes.

7 Teaching a Group Exercise Class

Vocabulary

- ▼ cognitive domain
- ▼ affective domain
- ▼ motor domain
- ▼ cognitive stage of learning
- ▼ associative stage of learning
- ▼ autonomous stage of learning
- ▼ program goals
- ▼ class objectives
- ▼ command style of teaching
- ▼ practice style of teaching
- ▼ reciprocal style of teaching
- ▼ self-check style of teaching
- ▼ inclusion style of teaching
- ▼ slow-to-fast strategy
- ▼ repetition reduction teaching strategy
- ▼ spatial teaching strategy
- ▼ part-to-whole teaching strategy
- ▼ simple-to-complex teaching strategy
- ▼ rhythm
- ▼ combinations
- ▼ beat
- ▼ downbeat
- ▼ meter
- ▼ measure
- ▼ accent
- ▼ tempo
- ▼ phrase
- ▼ freestyle choreography
- ▼ structured choreography
- ▼ linear progression
- ▼ physiological balance
- ▼ biomechanical balance
- ▼ psychological balance
- ▼ cueing
- ▼ feedback
- ▼ value statements

Getting Started

This chapter describes the fundamentals of teaching by reviewing the instructional design process, how people learn, and techniques for teaching and how they apply to group exercise. After completing this section you will have a better understanding of:

- ◆ the systematic design of instruction
- ◆ the needs of the exercise participant
- ◆ the stages of learning
- ◆ teaching strategies
- ◆ teaching styles
- ◆ the fundamentals of music
- ◆ class cues and visual cues
- ◆ how to evaluate performance

Reading Assignment

Read Chapter 7 of the *ACE Group Fitness Instructor Manual*, paying special attention to the words listed in the box to the left. After you have read the chapter, define these words on a separate piece of paper.

Expand Your Knowledge

I. Place the following steps in the instructional design process in the proper order.

a. _____ evaluating the quality of the class

b. _____ exercise selection

c. _____ understanding participant needs

d. _____ determining class goals and objectives

II. List the two questions necessary to perform an exercise evaluation for the following exercises.

a. hamstring stretch

1._____

2._____

b. biceps curl

1._____

2._____

c. grapevine with full turn

1._____

2._____

III. Match the descriptions on the right to the appropriate teaching style on the left.

1. command style of teaching

2. practice style of teaching

3. reciprocal style of teaching

4. self-check style of teaching

5. inclusion style of teaching

a. _____ the instructor makes all the decisions and the participants follow the instructor's directions and movements

b. _____ participants perform a given task and then record the results, comparing their results against given criteria or past performances

c. _____ involves the use of an observer or partner to provide feedback to each participant

d. _____ the instructor offers alternate positions for the different levels

e. _____ provides opportunities for individualization and includes private instructor feedback for each participant

IV. Fill in the space to the right of each letter by placing a (CD) if the statement describes the cognitive domain, an (AD) if the statement describes the affective domain, and an (MD) if the statement describes the motor domain.

a. _____ understanding injury prevention

b. _____ the love of cycling

c. _____ feeling out of shape

d. _____ moving through a full range of motion

e. _____ knowing the signs of overtraining

f. _____ keeping the abdominal muscles tight

V. List the three guidelines that will facilitate the movement of exercise participants from the beginner level to the advanced level.

a. _____

_____

b. _____

_____

c. _____

_____

VI. Match the descriptions on the left to the appropriate teaching strategy on the right.

a. _____ teach 8 right arm jabs, teach 4 double front kicks, reduce the number to 4 jabs and 2 double front kicks, reduce to 2 jabs and 1 double front

b. _____ teach 8 upper cuts, teach 8 side blocks, place them together in a combination; teach 16 alternating side kicks and add after the upper cuts and side blocks

c. _____ teach a side kick by giving 2 counts for the leg to chamber, 2 counts for the leg to extend, 2 counts for the leg to re-chamber, and 2 counts for the leg to return to the floor; reduce each part of the movement to single counts

d. _____ teach 8 right arm jabs, teach 4 front kicks, place them together in a combination; next time, modify the front kicks to double front kicks; next time, modify the jabs to alternate front and side

1. slow-to-fast

2. repetition reduction

3. part-to-whole

4. simple-to-complex

VII. What is the recommended music bpm for each of the following class segments?

a. _____ warm-up

b. _____ pre-stretches

c. _____ aerobic activities

d. _____ muscle conditioning

e. _____ post-stretching

VIII. Match the descriptions on the left to one of the six instructional design components on the right.

a. _____ what you expect students to gain from long-term participation

b. _____ determining which exercises are safe and effective to use in class

c. _____ becoming familiar with the health history and fitness level of each class member

d. _____ what you expect students to accomplish during each exercise session

e. _____ consists of class objectives, planned activities, necessary equipment, and time allotments

f. _____ formations used by instructors to provide their students with the maximum opportunities for learning and performance

1. participant needs

2. lesson plan

3. class objectives

4. exercise evaluation

5. program goals

6. patterns of class organization

IX. List the four guidelines for providing feedback.

1. _____

_____

2. _____

_____

3. _____

_____

4. _____

_____

X. Fill in the space to the right of each letter by placing a (I) if the movement is a level one movement, a (II) if the movement is a level two movement, a (III) if the movement is a level three movement, and a (IV) if the movement is a level four movement.

a. _____ grapevine

b. _____ knee lifts in place

c. _____ hamstring curls traveling forward

d. _____ step touch

e. _____ traveling knee lifts

f. _____ step touch traveling backward

Show What You Know

I. Create a verbal cue by placing the words into the correct order below the music counts provided.

a. press, side, arms, three, four, HUP!

Music Counts   1   2   3   4   5   6   7   8

b. front, tap, toe, four, three, clap

Music Counts   1   2   3   4   5   6   7   8

c. knee, lift, side, three, four

Music Counts   1   2   3   4   5   6   7   8

Practice What You Know

I. Evaluate an instructor's choreography by using the general guidelines for choreography found on pages 214–215 of the ACE Group Fitness Instructor Manual.

II. Create a sample lesson plan for a group fitness class. Be sure to include the class objectives, activities, time, patterns of class organization, equipment, music, and comments.

CHAPTER 8

Adherence and Motivation

Vocabulary

- adherence
- personal factors
- program factors
- environmental factors
- ratings of perceived exertion (RPE)
- feedback
- burnout
- eating disorders
- addictions
- dependence
- contract

Getting Started

This chapter describes the factors that affect exercise adherence, and strategies for helping participants develop positive attitudes and stay involved in regular exercise throughout their lives. After completing this section you will have a better understanding of:

- the basics of exercise adherence
- the major factors influencing exercise adherence
- seven traits of an ideal group fitness instructor
- leadership strategies that encourage exercise participation
- using exercise contracts and exercise logs
- the relationship between exercise and body image

Reading Assignment

Read Chapter 8 of the *ACE Group Fitness Instructor Manual*, paying special attention to the words listed in the box to the left. After you have read the chapter, define these words on a separate piece of paper.

Expand Your Knowledge

I. Place a (PER) next to the characteristics that most closely resemble a personal factor, a (PRO) next to the characteristics that most closely resemble a program factor, and an (ENV) next to the characteristics that most closely resemble an environmental factor.

a. _____ the length of time of the class

b. _____ starting and ending the class on time

c. _____ the posted time the class starts and ends

d. _____ competing demands on time

e. _____ family support

f. _____ physical coordination

II. Fill in the blanks.

a. The most common reasons for not continuing an exercise program are

_____ and _____.

b. About _____ % of American adults get the recommended amount of

physical activity.

c. Nearly _____ % of those who start an exercise program drop out within the

first six months.

d. When considering effectively increasing fitness levels, _____

performed throughout the day is just as effective as a single 30-minute

exercise bout.

III. Match the support types on the right with the description on the left.

a. _____ challenge to make goals and achieve them

b. _____ feedback on goal achievements

c. _____ sympathetic to struggles with starting exercise

d. _____ sounding board for communication experiences associated with exercise

e. _____ information associated with exercise

f. _____ exercise partner; set and work on goals together

g. _____ comfort and reassurance when goals are not met; reward givers when goals are met

1. listeners

2. experts

3. appraisers

4. affection providers

5. role models/partners

6. emotional providers

7. challengers

IV. Provide an example of how a group fitness instructor can encourage adherence for each participant's behavior.

a. new participant expects to lose 10 pounds (4.5 kg) a month for the next

three months _____

_____

b. during class, some participants are exercising excessively

_____

_____

c. a participant is having difficulty accepting his or her own body shape

_____

_____

d. a participant is going to the beach for a two-week vacation

_____

_____

V. List the four signs of exercise dependence/ addiction.

1. _____

_____

_____

2. _____

_____

_____

3. _____

_____

_____

4. _____

_____

_____

VI. Describe the necessary steps when dealing with excessive complainers.

_____

_____

_____

_____

_____

VII. Considering a new or beginning participant, describe the major differences between the following pairs of words or phrases.

a. an RPE level of 11 and an RPE level of 16 _____

_____

_____

b. short-term goals and long-term goals _____

_____

_____

c. extrinsic rewards and intrinsic rewards _____

_____

_____

d. transient discomforts associated with exercise and discomforts that are

potential signs of injury _____

_____

_____

Show What You Know

I. *A teenage exercise partici-*
pant, Nikki, is always
smoking a cigarette out-
side of the gym as you
arrive. List the appropri-
ate instructor strategy and
explain the rationale.
Give an example of appro-
priate feedback.

strategy: _____

_____

rationale: _____

_____

feedback: _____

_____

II. *Your exercise class does*
not appear to be cohesive;
each person keeps to them-
selves. List the appropriate
instructor strategy and
explain the rationale.
Give an example of an
appropriate ice-breaker.

strategy: _____

_____

rationale: _____

_____

ice-breaker: _____

_____

Practice What You Know

I. *Fill out a sample exercise*
contract (page 236) for a
beginner participant.

II. *Fill out a sample exercise*
log (page 237) for one
week.

Vocabulary

- obesity
- osteoporosis
- body mass index (BMI)
- overweight
- type 2 diabetes
- osteoarthritis
- low-back pain
- neuropathy
- type 1 diabetes
- insulin
- glucometer
- insulin reaction
- insulin shock
- chronic obstructive pulmonary disease (COPD)
- asthma
- chronic bronchitis
- emphysema
- exercise-induced asthma (EIA)
- peak flow meter
- beta adrenergic stimulating agent
- dyspnea
- diaphragmatic breathing
- rheumatoid arthritis
- kyphosis
- dowager's hump
- multiple sclerosis

Getting Started

This chapter provides an overview of the major disabilities and health limitations you are likely to encounter, and modifications to basic exercise programs that can help participants with varying degrees of disabling conditions to maintain a healthy lifestyle. After completing this section you will have a better understanding of:

- ◆ guidelines for persons with obesity
- ◆ exercising with diabetes
- ◆ respiratory and pulmonary disorders
- ◆ joint and bone disorders
- ◆ guidelines for persons with physical disabilities
- ◆ exercising and multiple sclerosis
- ◆ coronary heart disease

Reading Assignment

Read Chapter 9 of the *ACE Group Fitness Instructor Manual,* paying special attention to the words listed in the box to the left. After you have read the chapter, define these words on a separate piece of paper.

Expand Your Knowledge

I. Describe the major difference in the following pairs of words or phrases.

a. hemorrhagic strokes and ischemic strokes _____

_____

b. hypoglycemia and hyperglycemia _____

_____

c. blood glucose lower than 100 mg/dL and blood glucose greater than 300 mg/dL

_____

d. exercise intensity for a young person with asthma and exercise intensity for

older individuals with asthma _____

_____

e. diaphragmatic breathing and pursed-lip breathing _____

_____

II. List the six exercise guidelines for obesity.

1. _____

_____

2. _____

_____

3. _____

_____

4. _____

_____

5. _____

_____

6. _____

_____

III. Fill in the space to the right of each letter by placing an (ES) if the condition describes an early symptom of insulin reaction and an (LS) if the condition describes a late symptom of insulin reaction.

a. _____ insomnia

b. _____ nausea

c. _____ pale, moist skin

d. _____ extreme hunger

e. _____ strong, rapid pulse

f. _____ headache

IV. List the three steps for managing an asthma attack.

1. _____

_____

2. _____

_____

3. _____

_____

V. Describe the Americans with Disabilities Act.

_____

_____

_____

_____

_____

_____

_____

_____

VI. Describe the guidelines for weight training for persons with osteoporosis.

a. repetitions _____

_____

b. sets _____

_____

c. frequency_____

_____

VII. Explain how you would modify the exercise in the following cases.

a. a person with arthritis experiencing pain in their shoulder when performing

chest flyes _____

_____

_____

b. a person with multiple sclerosis with worsening balance working with free

weights _____

_____

_____

c. a person with osteoporosis swimming to increase bone density

_____

_____

d. an obese person uncomfortable with the standard bike seat and setting

_____

_____

VIII. What is the major concern when working with persons with coronary heart disease?

_____

_____

_____

_____

_____

_____

_____

_____

Show What You Know

I. For each condition, indicate the best choice of exercise programming and explain your rationale.

a. arthritis: total-body elliptical machine or stair climber

_____

_____

b. osteoarthritis: wake-up workout or lunch-time workout

_____

_____

c. multiple sclerosis: cool-water swimming or warm-water swimming

_____

_____

d. persons with coronary heart disease: circuit training or steady-state training

_____

_____

II. An obese beginning exerciser wants to take your Super Fatburner Class that is offered three days per week. The class is 90 minutes long with high-impact aerobics, stepping, and weight training. What do you recommend to the student?

_____

_____

_____

_____

_____

_____

Practice What You Know

Evaluate your facility based on its accessibility to persons with disabilities. There are two important risks involved in this exercise: injury due to a fall and offending others by acting unprofessional. Access a wheel chair and have another individual help you to avoid injury. To simulate visual impairment, tie a bandanna over your eyes and have another individual help you to avoid injury. Attempt your normal workout from beginning to end.

10 *Exercise and Pregnancy*

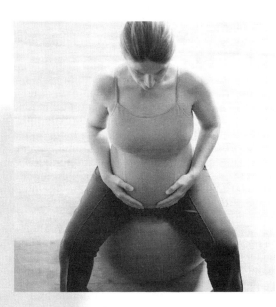

Vocabulary

- ▼ fetus
- ▼ postpartum
- ▼ tachycardia
- ▼ relaxin
- ▼ progesterone
- ▼ supine hypotension
- ▼ hypoxia
- ▼ thermoregulation
- ▼ hematocrit
- ▼ placenta
- ▼ hyperthermia
- ▼ teratogenic
- ▼ pelvic floor
- ▼ diastasis recti
- ▼ sciatica
- ▼ vascular disturbances
- ▼ transient osteoporosis
- ▼ sphincter
- ▼ perineal
- ▼ incontinence
- ▼ Kegel exercises
- ▼ symphysis pubis
- ▼ estrogen
- ▼ broad ligaments
- ▼ inguinal ligament
- ▼ round ligament

Getting Started

This chapter describes the physiological adaptations that occur during pregnancy and postpartum, as well as appropriate program suggestions and modifications. After completing this section, you should have a better understanding of:

- ◆ the benefits of exercise during pregnancy
- ◆ contraindications for pregnant participants
- ◆ physiological adaptations to pregnancy
- ◆ fetal risks associated with exercise
- ◆ special concerns for pregnant participants and program modifications
- ◆ postnatal exercise and spotting tips

Reading Assignment

Read Chapter 10 of the *ACE Group Fitness Instructor Manual,* paying special attention to the words listed in the box to the left. After you have read the chapter, define these words on a separate piece of paper.

Expand Your Knowledge

I. Select the symptoms you believe indicate the need to cease exercise and consult the participant's physician immediately by marking them with an (X).

_____ a. uterine contractions occurring every 30 minutes

_____ b. visual disturbances

_____ c. decreased fetal activity

_____ d. sweating at the onset of exercise

_____ e. shortness of breath

II. Describe the major differences between the following pairs of words or phrases.

a. absolute contraindication and relative contraindication_____

_____

_____

b. lordotic curve and kyphotic curve_____

_____

_____

c. birth weights in moderately active athletes and birth weights in athletes that

maintain or increase their exercise in late pregnancy _____

_____

_____

d. fetal temperature and maternal temperature_____

_____

_____

III. List the three contributors to diastis recti.

1. _____

_____

2. _____

_____

3. _____

_____

IV. Compare a pregnant woman who exercises to one who does not exercise. Place a (↑) next to the areas that tend to be higher for pregnant women who exercise, a (↓) for those areas that tend to be lower for pregnant women who exercise, and a (←→) for those areas that remain the same in exercisers and non-exercisers.

a. _____ oxygen and nutrient delivery to baby

b. _____ confidence in body image

c. _____ duration of labor

d. _____ irritation of the pubic symphysis

e. _____ lung space

f. _____ fasting blood glucose levels

g. _____ symptoms of postpartum depression

h. _____ quality or quantity of breast milk

V. Fill in the blanks.

a. The most frequent complaint during pregnancy is _____.

b. The _____ trimester is most crucial in the formation of the fetus.

c. The most common nerve problem during pregnancy is _____

_____.

d. Average pregnancy weight gain is between _____ and _____ pounds.

e. The suggested time for returning to group exercise activities is after the

participant's postpartum doctor appointment, or _____.

VI. For each of the following exercises, explain how they might be modified to accommodate a second trimester pregnant participant.

a. supine abdominal curls _____

_____

_____

b. prone hip extension_____

_____

_____

c. lying hip abduction _____

_____

_____

d. flexibility exercises _____

_____

_____

VII. List the three fetal risks associated with exercise and describe the potential concern.

1. _____

concern: _____

_____

2. _____

concern: _____

_____

3. _____

concern: _____

_____

VIII. Describe the typical posture of a pregnant woman. Explain the areas that require stretching and the areas that require strengthening to support proper alignment.

a. posture _____

_____

_____

b. stretching exercises _____

_____

_____

c. strengthening exercises _____

_____

_____

IX. Match the musculoskeletal dysfunctions and irritations on the right to the descriptions on the left.

a. _____ the linea alba widens and finally gives way to the mechanical stress of an advancing pregnancy

b. _____ a pain felt at the sacroiliac joint, which then radiates into the buttocks

c. _____ irritation at the sacroiliac joint and the hip joint

d. _____ a pain that radiates from the buttocks down to the legs

e. _____ irritation of the pubic symphysis

1. pelvic floor weakness

2. sciatica

3. sacroiliac joint dysfunction

4. pubic pain

5. diastasis recti

Show What You Know

I. *Describe how you would modify your indoor cycling class to create a safe and effective exercise class for a pregnant student. The participant is a regular exerciser who informed you of the pregnancy at six weeks and is exercising through the pregnancy. It is the summer and very hot.*

_____

_____

_____

_____

_____

II. *A student who is pregnant with twins shows up to class extremely tired, cranky, hungry, and has a headache. What could be the problem and what would you recommend?*

_____

_____

_____

_____

_____

III. *A student is returning to the gym after meeting with her primary care provider, who recommended a conservative approach to abdominal strengthening due to her wide separation at the abdominal wall. Provide her with an exercise progression for her abdominals.*

_____

_____

_____

_____

Practice What You Know

Observe a prenatal exercise class and review the instructor guidelines that begin on page 292.

11 *Injury Prevention and Emergency Procedures*

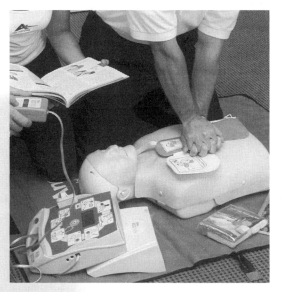

Getting Started

This chapter describes most of the common musculoskeletal injuries associated with group fitness classes, methods of injury prevention including appropriate modifications for specific injuries, and emergency procedures for responding to them. After completing this section you will have a better understanding of:

- ◆ symptoms and types of musculoskeletal injuries
- ◆ the factors associated with injury
- ◆ sprains, strains, and tendinitis
- ◆ specific musculoskeletal injuries
- ◆ emergency plans and procedures

Vocabulary

- ▼ contraindications
- ▼ sprain
- ▼ strain
- ▼ plantar fasciitis
- ▼ stress fractures
- ▼ acute injury
- ▼ tendinitis
- ▼ ligament
- ▼ fractures
- ▼ tendon
- ▼ plyometric
- ▼ prognosis
- ▼ RICE
- ▼ proprioception
- ▼ tennis elbow
- ▼ chondromalacia
- ▼ low-back pain
- ▼ supine
- ▼ vital signs

Reading Assignment

Read Chapter 11 of the *ACE Group Fitness Instructor Manual,* paying special attention to the words listed in the box to the left. After you have read the chapter, define these words on a separate piece of paper.

Expand Your Knowledge

I. List the three injury-related responsibilities of group fitness instructors.

1. _____

_____

_____

2. _____

_____

_____

3. _____

_____

_____

II. Fill in the space to the right of each letter by placing an (A) if the description characterizes an acute injury or a (C) if the description characterizes a chronic injury.

a. _____ linked to a specific event

b. _____ inadequate amounts of recovery between exercise sessions

c. _____ usually of gradual onset

d. _____ symptoms are sharply defined

e. _____ stress fractures and tennis elbow

f. _____ direct diagnosis may be more difficult

g. _____ broken leg or wrist sprain

III. Match the musculoskeletal injury on the right with the symptoms on the left.

a. _____ damage to the anterior talofibular ligament

b. _____ affects the wrist extensor muscles at the lateral epicondyle of the humerus

c. _____ microtearing of the attachment of the muscles of the lower leg on the tibia

d. _____ caused by a direct blow to the knee or knee hyperextension

e. _____ stretching of the anterior capsule and ligaments that allows the humeral head to sublux or dislocate anteriorly

f. _____ microtearing near the calcaneus bone

g. _____ affects the wrist flexor muscles at the medial epicondyle of the humerus

1. shin splints

2. plantar fasciitis

3. lateral ankle sprain

4. tennis elbow

5. anterior shoulder instability

6. anterior crucial ligament tear

7. golfer's elbow

IV. Describe the major differences between the following pairs of words or phrases.

a. rotator cuff strain and rotator cuff impingement _____

_____

_____

b. sprain and strain _____

_____

_____

c. musculoskeletal injury as it relates to group fitness instructors and

musculoskeletal injury as it relates to healthcare providers _____

_____

_____

V. List the five symptoms of injury.

1. _____

_____

2. _____

_____

3. _____

_____

4. _____

_____

5. _____

_____

VI. Indicate the proper order for each step during an emergency response.

a. _____ clean area appropriately

b. _____ assign someone to control the crowd and alert the other facility locations of the situation

c. _____ send someone to call emergency services

d. _____ evaluate the victim/situation

e. _____ complete the necessary documentation

f. _____ continue to provide necessary victim support until emergency personnel arrive

g. _____ get the automated external defibrillator (AED)

VII. *Describe the concerns related to the following factors associated with injury.*

a. concrete floor _____

_____

b. carpeted floor _____

_____

c. lateral movement and footwear _____

_____

d. incorporating movements from other disciplines into class _____

_____

VIII. *Match the specific musculoskeltal injury on the right with the consideration for group exercise on the left. In some cases, more than one response may be appropriate.*

a. _____ avoid repetitive impact on hard surfaces

b. _____ encourage stretching the posterior cuff and discourage stretching the anterior shoulder

c. _____ avoid full squats or excessive knee flexion

d. _____ use lighter loads for the wrist during repetitive motion

e. _____ double-check that participants are wearing footwear appropriate for the class

f. _____ avoid pivoting

1. anterior shoulder instability

2. anterior cruciate ligament tear

3. patellofemoral pain disorders

4. shin splints

5. plantar fasciitis

6. lateral ankle sprain

7. lateral epicondylitis

8. rotator cuff impingement

IX. *List the four guidelines that can be used to provide modifications for movement for participants with low-back pain.*

1. _____

_____

2. _____

_____

3. _____

_____

4. _____

_____

Show What You Know

I. Describe the types of exercise modifications you may need to provide during class given the following class situation.

a. new participants in a low-impact class _____

_____

_____

b. an individual with tendinitis during a group strength training class _____

_____

_____

c. active 80-year-olds in an aquatic exercise class _____

_____

_____

II. Case Analysis: Analyze the following situation and describe what recommendations you should make should you become aware of the situation (a) prior to class, (b) during class, or (c) after class.

You are teaching a group cycling class at a tennis facility. What are some modifications you can make for Johnny Lobb and Frankie Volley, both of whom are suffering from tennis elbow?

a. _____

_____

b. _____

_____

c. _____

_____

Practice What You Know

Write out an emergency plan for the medical emergencies you are likely to encounter. Be sure to create an emergency plan for each facility, as phone numbers and access information will be different. You can use the information as a reference, to role play, or to review as needed.

12 *Legal and Professional Responsibilities*

Vocabulary

- ▼ liability
- ▼ standard of care
- ▼ negligence
- ▼ defendant
- ▼ plaintiff
- ▼ risk management
- ▼ statute of limitations
- ▼ general liability insurance
- ▼ professional liability insurance
- ▼ disability insurance
- ▼ individual medical insurance
- ▼ waiver
- ▼ informed consent
- ▼ assumption-of-risk
- ▼ contracts
- ▼ independent contractor
- ▼ copyright
- ▼ public performance
- ▼ performing rights societies
- ▼ blanket license
- ▼ publisher
- ▼ compilations
- ▼ Americans with Disabilities Act
- ▼ scope of practice

Getting Started

This chapter is designed to explain the legal issues and areas of responsibility that concern group fitness instructors. These concepts can be used to reduce the likelihood that an instructor or studio owner will be involved in a lawsuit. After completing this section you will have a better understanding of:

- ◆ the areas of responsibility and guidelines for group fitness instructors

- ◆ accident reporting

- ◆ selection of response for risks

- ◆ risk-management systems

- ◆ the basic defenses against negligence claims

- ◆ the difference between independent contractors and employees

Reading Assignment

Read Chapter 12 of the *ACE Group Fitness Instructor Manual*, paying special attention to the words listed in the box to the left. After you have read the chapter, define these words on a separate piece of paper.

Expand Your Knowledge

I. Describe the major differences between the following pairs of words and phrases.

a. defendant and plaintiff _____

_____

_____

b. contributory negligence and comparative negligence _____

_____

_____

c. acts of omission and acts of commission _____

_____

_____

d. waiver and informed consent _____

_____

_____

II. List the four elements necessary to legally substantiate a charge of negligence.

1. _____

_____

2. _____

_____

3. _____

_____

4. _____

_____

III. *Match the following conditions to the most appropriate type of insurance coverage by filling in the space to the right of each letter with (GL) if it may be covered by general liability insurance, (PL) if it may be covered by professional liability insurance, (DI) if it may be covered by disability insurance, and (IM) if it may be covered by individual medical insurance.*

a. _____ the instructor can't teach for six weeks due to a stress fracture

b. _____ hospital bills associated with a stress fracture

c. _____ an exercise participant slips on the ice outside of the health club

d. _____ an instructor slips on the ice outside of the health club

e. _____ medical costs associated with a pregnancy

f. _____ a participant sues the instructor for an injury sustained during class

IV. *For each of the following situations, describe how you could lower your risk of being found legally responsible if an injury occurred.*

a. A student places her water bottle and towel to the side of the step during

the warm-up. _____

_____

_____

b. The exercise bands are old, sticky, and have nicks in them. _____

_____

_____

c. Prior to class, a new participant informs you he has had heart surgery.

_____

_____

d. Your facility wants you to teach a Pilates class in three months. You have

never taught Pilates. _____

_____

_____

V. Determine whether each of the following statements describes work conditions normally associated with either an independent contractor or an employee. Place a (C) next to the statements that meet the conditions for independent contractor status. Place an (E) next to the statements that meet the conditions for employee status.

_____ a. you provide all the equipment for the class

_____ b. you receive a single payment for eight weeks of classes

_____ c. you are hired to teach a Wednesday class indefinitely

_____ d. the employer provides training on a regular basis

_____ e. you teach a lunch-time class for an insurance agency

_____ f. the employer has a high level of control over the details of the class

VI. Match the term on the left with its guideline on the right.

_____ a. health screening

_____ b. programming

_____ c. instruction

_____ d. supervision

_____ e. facilities

_____ f. equipment

1. floor surface is appropriate for each activity

2. conformance to standard of care

3. evaluation is conducted prior to participating in exercise

4. a schedule of regular service and repair is established and documented

5. health history is used appropriately in program design

6. continuous supervision is provided in immediate proximity to the participant to ensure safety

VII. List the four basic defenses against negligence claims.

1. _____

_____

2. _____

_____

3. _____

_____

4. _____

_____

VIII. Select those statements you believe fall within the scope of practice of a group fitness instructor by marking them with an (X).

_____ a. using the results of an exercise test to create a program to treat shortness of breath

_____ b. reviewing the MyPyramid Food Guidance System with a healthy participant

_____ c. recommending exercise to help someone get through a tough divorce

_____ d. explaining to a participant how you select your own shoes

Show What You Know

I. *Case study: Consider the following situation and describe (a) What do you do for the participant? and (b) What do you do for the club?*

A participant who is five months pregnant is performing supine abdominal curls. When you question her about it, she says that another instructor, Kit, explained that she performed the exercise until her sixth month. She also states that she has not talked it over with her physician.

_____

_____

_____

_____

_____

_____

II. *Case Analysis: Analyze the following situation and determine if the four elements exist to legally substantiate the charge of negligence.*

A participant breaks her leg while following instructions during a step class. The participant was treated by a physician and documented the injury. The movement that led to the injury was a reverse turn step, which involves stepping backward onto the step and is considered a blind move, or a move in which you cannot see the step. Blind moves are not recommended by the manufacturer of the product used during step class.

1._____

_____

2._____

_____

3._____

_____

4._____

_____

Practice What You Know

Perform a risk-management assessment to evaluate the risk of injury at your facility using the guidelines found in this chapter.

Appendix A

Certification Information Guide

I. Purpose
The purpose of this information is to provide you with insight into the American Council on Exercise's (ACE) certification process. By understanding how the examination is developed, we believe you can better prepare for the exam. ACE follows the highest standards for professional and occupational certification tests, taking measures to uphold validity, reliability, and fairness for all candidates in our examinations.

II. How is the Exam developed?
The ACE certification examinations are developed by ACE and volunteer committees of experts in the field(s) in cooperation with CASTLE Worldwide, Inc., an independent testing agency. The exam development process involves the following steps:

A. Job Analysis
A committee of experts in the fitness field thoroughly analyzes the job requirements and develops an outline of the knowledge and skills necessary to perform the job competently.

B. Validation Study
A research survey is then conducted to determine if the job analysis is valid. This survey is sent to thousands of randomly selected fitness professionals for input and validation. The final outcome is the *Exam Content Outline*. (See Appendix B in the *ACE Group Fitness Instructor Manual*).

C. Item Writing
A national panel of experts develops questions for the exam. Questions are tied specifically to the validated *Exam Content Outline,* which resulted from the job analysis. All questions are also referenced to an acceptable text or document and further validated for importance, criticalness, and relevance. CASTLE then reviews the questions for the degree to which they adhere to testing guidelines.

D. Exam Construction
The questions are then reviewed in detail one more time by the examination committee before being placed on the final exam forms.

E. Cut Score Determination
Once the final exam is constructed, the exam committee rates the difficulty of each question and the passing point is then determined by statistical analysis of the committee ratings. This analysis adjusts for variability in the ratings and gives benefit to the test candidate.

F. Continual Exam Evaluation
Once the exam process is completed, continual evaluation and analysis of each question help to ensure validity. The examination is revised each year with items being reworked or replaced. Approximately every five years the exam-development process begins again with a new job analysis.

III. How is the Exam administered?
An independent testing agency is used to administer all ACE examinations to ensure exam security, integrity, and the elimination of bias. Be assured that all of the policies that ACE follows concerning exam administration are required to maintain these high standards.

IV. Who is eligible to take the Exam?
Anyone who is at least 18 years of age and has a valid CPR certification is eligible to take the ACE certification exam. For the ACE Group Fitness Instructor Certification Examination it is assumed that the examinee will be competent in the areas described in the *Exam Content Outline* found in Appendix B of the *ACE Group Fitness Instructor Manual*. For information concerning fees, registration procedures, and testing dates and sites, please visit the ACE Web site at www.acefitness.org. Or contact ACE at the following address for an Exam Information Brochure.

American Council on Exercise
4851 Paramount Drive
San Diego, CA 92123
(800) 825-3636
www.acefitness.org

Answer Key

Chapter One:
Exercise Physiology

Expand Your Knowledge

I. (a) 4, (b) 5, (c) 2, (d) 1, (e) 3

II. (a) C, (b) F, C, P, (c) P, (d) F, (e) P, (f) C

III. (a) Anaerobic glycolysis occurs without the presence of oxygen. Aerobic glycolysis occurs with oxygen and results in a larger amount of ATP.
(b) In a concentric contraction the muscle shortens when stimulated. In an eccentric contraction the muscle lengthens when it is stimulated.
(c) Static stretching involves holding a static (nonmoving) position. Ballistic stretching is characterized by bobbing or bouncing.
(d) Systolic blood pressure is a function of the force generated by the heart during its contraction. Diastolic blood pressure is a measure of the pressure in the arteries during the relaxation phase of the heart cycle.
(e) Exercise for type 2 diabetes enables carbohydrates to be used more effectively, promotes weight loss, and is rarely dangerous or difficult. Exercise for type 1 diabetes is much more complex.
(f) Vasoconstriction is the contraction of the arterioles. Vasodilation is the relaxation of the arterioles.
(g) Sensory neurons convey electrical impulses from the periphery to the CNS. Motor neurons convey electrical impulses from the CNS to the periphery.

IV. (1) Begin exercising in the heat gradually; (2) Always wear lightweight, well-ventilated clothing; (3) Never wear impermeable or non-breathable garments; (4) Replace body fluids as they are lost; (5) Recording daily body weight is an excellent way to prevent accumulative dehydration.

V. (a) FT, (b) ST, (c) ST, (d) FT, (e) ST

VI. (1) Wear several layers of clothing; (2) Allow for adequate ventilation of sweat; (3) Select garments that allow the body to give off body heat during exercise and retain body heat during inactive periods; (4) Replace body fluids in the cold, just as in the heat.

VII. (a) EPOC, (b) DEF, (c) EPOC, (d) SS, (e) DEF

VIII. (a) 6, (b) 8, (c) 2, (d) 7, (e) 5, (f) 1, (g) 3, (h) 4

IX. (a) CO = SV x HR; (b) ADP + Energy from CP + P —> ATP; (c) GLU —> ATP + LA.

X. (1) Exercise intensity should be approximately 50-85% of maximal oxygen consumption ($\dot{V}O_2$max) or HR reserve; (2) Exercise duration should be a minimum of 10 minutes per session with a goal of at least 20 minutes of aerobic activity accumulated each day; (3) Exercise frequency should be at least three days per week.

XI. (a) Myosin and actin are myofilaments within muscle that create muscle shortening; (b) Lactic acid rapidly accumulates when exceeding anaerobic threshold; (c) A slight warm-up period should precede stretching exercises; (d) Stretching exercises may help reduce DOMS.

Show What You Know

I. Participants may experience altitude sickness. Signs and symptoms of altitude sickness include shortness of breath, headache, lightheadedness, and nausea. Keep exercise intensity light, incorporate shorter, more frequent sessions, and use prolonged warm-ups and cool-downs for the first two to three days as participants become acclimatized to altitude.

II. (CO = SV x HR); 125 ml O_2/beat x 200 beats/min = 25,000 ml O_2/min

Chapter Two:
Fundamentals of Anatomy

Expand Your Knowledge

Section 1: Anatomy

I. (a) 1, (b) 3, (c) 4, (d) 7, (e) 8, (f) 2, (g) 5, (h) 6

II. (a) Arteries carry blood away from the heart. Veins transport blood toward the heart.
(b) The axial skeleton is composed of the 80 bones that make up the head, neck, and trunk. The appendicular skeleton is composed of the 126 bones that form the extremities.
(c) The periosteum is the connective tissue sheath on the outer surface of the diaphysis of a long bone. The endosteum is a soft tissue lining on the internal surface of the diaphysis.
(d) Oxygen is required for energy production and cellular activity. Carbon dioxide is a by-product of energy production and cellular activity.
(e) The stretch reflex should be avoided during stretching by performing stretches slowly and controlled. The GTO reflex is a desired response during stretching that permits additional range of motion.

III. (1) a, superior vena cava; (7) b, pulmonary veins; (2) c, right atrium; (4) d, pulmonary valve; (3) e, right ventricle; (1) f, inferior vena cava; (11) g, aorta; (6) h, right and left pulmonary arteries; (5) i, pulmonary trunk; (8) j, left atrium; (9) k, mitral valve; (10) l, left ventricle

IV. (a) renal artery, (b) external jugular vein, (c) radial artery, (d) pulmonary vein, (e) aortic arch

V. (a) C, (b) E, (c) C, (d) I, (e) E, (f) I

VI. (a) cervical plexus, innervates the head, neck, upper chest, and shoulders, (b) brachial plexus, innervates from the shoulders all the way down to the hand, (c) lumbar plexus, innervates the abdomen, groin, genitalia, and anterolateral aspects of the thigh, (d) sacral plexus, innervates the larger muscles of the posterior thigh and the entire lower leg, ankle, and foot

VII. (1) protection for vital organs, (2) support for soft tissue, (3) provides a framework of levers to produce movement, (4) the production of blood cells, (5) storage of calcium and other minerals

VIII. (a) F, (b) C, (c) C, (d) S, (e) S, (f) F, (g) S

IX. (a) long bones are those in which the length exceeds the width and thickness, (b) short bones are approximately equal in length and width, (c) flat bones are thin and usually bent or curved rather than flat, (d) irregular bones are bones of various shapes that do not fall into these other categories

X. (a) S, 6, (b) F, 5, (c) T, 4, (d) F, 1, (e) F, 7, (f) S, 8, (g) F, 2, (h) F, 3

XI. See Figures 2.19a & b, 2.21, 2.22, 2.26, 2.28, 2.30, 2.32

XII. (a) triceps brachii, (b) trapezius, levator scapula, rhomboid major and minor, (c) anterior tibialis, (d) gluteus medius and minimus, (e) transverse abdominis, (f) erector spinae

Chapter Three: Fundamentals of Applied Kinesiology

I. SITS = an acronym to recall the four muscles of the rotator cuff group; S = supraspinatus, I = infraspinatus, T = teres minor, and S = subscapularis

II. (a) Law of Acceleration, (b) Law of Inertia, (c) Law of Reaction

III. (1) the sternoclavicular joint (S/C), (2) the acromioclavicular joint (A/C), (3) the glenohumeral joint (G/H), (4) the scapulothoracic articulation (S/T)

IV. (a) hamstrings (biceps femoris, semitendinosus, and semimembranosus) and gluteus maximus, (b) quadriceps femoris (vastus lateralis, vastus medialis, vastus intermedius, and the rectus femoris), (c) soleus and gastrocnemius, (d) the three gluteal muscles (gluteus medius, gluteus minimus, and the superior fibers of the gluteus maximus)

V. (a) Lordosis is an increased anterior lumbar curve (lower). Kyphosis is an increased posterior thoracic curve (higher). (b) The external obliques are superficial and run diagonally downward and forward. The internal obliques are deep and run diagonally downward and posteriorly. (c) Retraction is adduction of the scapula. Protraction is abduction of the scapula. (d) Concentric contraction of the upper trapezius produces elevation and adduction. Concentric retraction of the lower trapezius produces depression and adduction.

VI. (1) bilateral symmetry, equal strength and flexibility on the right and left sides of the body, (2) proportional strength ratios in opposing (agonist/antagonist) muscle groups, (3) a balance of flexibility, not to exceed normal ranges

VII. (a) trapezius, rhomboids, and levator scapulae, (b) pectoralis major, deltoid, rotator cuff, latissimus dorsi, and teres major, (c) pectoralis minor and serratus anterior

VIII. (a) 3, (b) 2, (c) 6, (d) 1, (e) 4, (f) 5

IX. (a) knee flexion beyond 90 degrees with weights may strain the knee; reduce the squat to 90 degrees or less, or remove any added weight, (b) may contribute to low-back pain; strengthen the client's abdominals and hip extensors while stretching the hip flexors and spine extensors, (c) abduction combined with internal rotation may strain the rotator cuff muscles; move the weight to a point in front of the body, (d) hip abduction will only work a portion of the gluteus maximus; perform a hip extension exercise.

Chapter Four: Introduction to Nutrition

Expand Your Knowledge

I. (a) C, P, (b) P, (c) C, (d) F, (e) F

II. (a) Viscous fibers form a gel with fluids in the gut and bowel and speed the digestive process. Incompletely fermented fibers do not tend to bind with water and slow the digestive process. (b) Simple carbohydrates contain fruit, milk, and refined sugars. Complex carbohydrates are made up of longer chains of carbon atoms. (c) Essential amino acids must be provided in the diet. Non-essential amino acids are manufactured by the body. (d) Low-density lipoproteins are involved in the artery blocking process. High-density lipoproteins are involved in moving body lipids from places of storage to places of use. (e) Saturated fats have no double bonds and are mostly solid at room temperature. Unsaturated fats have at least one carbon-carbon double bond and are liquid at room temperature.

III. (1) Increase intake of whole grain breads and cereals. (2) Choose foods with as little processing as possible. (3) Include several servings of fresh fruits and vegetables daily. (4) Include legumes in your diet on a regular basis. (5) Consume moderate amounts of meat.

IV. (a) intake: 50-60% of total calories; function: main energy fuel for body, brain, and CNS. (b) intake:10-15% of total calories; function: makes up structural components like muscles, skin, tendons, organs, and bones. (c) intake: 25-30% of total calories; function: energy storage, cushion vital organs, insulation, and basic functions. (d) intake: a person consuming 2,000 kcal/day needs about 2–3 liters (7 to 11 cups); functions: regulates body temperature, maintains blood pressure, delivers nutrients, and removes waste. (e) intake: 25–35 g/day; functions: regulates speed of digestion, regulates cholesterol levels. (f) intake: 300 mg or less per day; function: basic unit for many cells and hormones in the body.

V. (a) BN, (b) AN, (c) AN, BN, (d) BED, (e) AN, BN, BED

VI. (a) A high dietary fat intake is associated with increased rates of CVD. (b) A high intake of sodium can aggravate blood pressure in about 40% of hypertensive individuals. (c) Body builders and other participants may spend enormous sums of money to build muscle using protein powders. However, they are not necessary if a healthy diet is maintained. (d) Caffeine stimulates the central nervous system and may act as a diuretic, but has no conclusive benefit to exercisers/athletes. (e) Phytochemicals are believed to reduce the body's risk for a variety of different cancers.

VII. (a) 80, (b) A, D, E, K, (c) C, B1, B2, Niacin, B6, B12, Folic acid, pantothenic acid, and biotin, (d) 15

Show What You Know

I. 10 kcal x 132 lb = 1,320 kcal/day

II. Deficiency/Problem: She is at risk of calcium deficiency, which can lead to osteoporosis. Recommendations: Work with a registered dietitian to supplement calcium.

III. Total kcal necessary to lose 10 lb:
(10 lb x 3,500 kcal/lb = 35,000 kcal)
3,500 kcal/2 weeks = 1,750 kcal per week
Therefore, 35,000 kcal total / 1,750 kcal/week = 20 weeks

Chapter Five: Health Screening

Expand Your Knowledge

I. (a) classifies a potential exercise participant according to disease risk, and facilitates the exercise programming process, (b) identifies those in need of a referral to a healthcare provider for more extensive evaluation, ensures the safety of exercise testing and participation, and determines the appropriate exercise test or program, (c) determines the safety of initiating an exercise program and provides specific recommendations for exercise training, including heart-rate limits during exercise

II. (1) L, (2) M, (3) H, (4) M, (5) L

III. (a) 30–50%, (b) one-third, (c) 10, (d) one-quarter

IV. (1) men, (2) sedentary, (3) over the age of 35, (4) already had heart disease or were at high risk for it, (5) exercised too hard for their fitness levels

V. See chart above.

VI. (a) NR, (b) NR, (c) ME, ET, (d) ME, ET, (e) NR

VII. (a) The AHA is encouraging competitive athletes to undergo cardiovascular screening prior to participation in sports to reduce the number of sudden deaths among athletes. (b) Middle-aged/elderly participants are the fastest growing segment in health/fitness facilities. (c) Health screening identifies individuals who need medical clearance to begin an exercise program.

Show What You Know

I. (a) The next step is to contact Kara's physician and explain the results of the health screening. Before Kara can undergo a fitness appraisal or begin an exercise program, she needs approval from a physician. A medical release form should be sent along with the physician referral form. (b) Kara's exercising heart rate will be lower due to the beta-adrenergic channel blockers.

II. Now that Everett is 46 years old, he has moved from the low risk–stratification category to the moderate risk–stratification category. It is recommended that he either lower his intensity to 11–13 on the ratings of perceived exertion (RPE) scale or have a medical exam and an exercise test before exercising at a higher intensity.

Medications	Resting HR	Exercising HR	Exercise Performance
Antihistamines	←→	←→	←→
Antihypertensives	↑ ←→ ↓	↑ ←→ ↓	←→
Beta-adrenergic blocking agents	↓	↓	↓ ←→
Caffeine	←→ ↑	←→ ↑	←→ ↑
Calcium channel blockers	↑ ←→ ↓	↑ ←→ ↓	↓ ←→
Diuretics	←→	←→	←→

Chapter Six: Group Exercise Program Design

Expand Your Knowledge

I. (a) Methods or principles for successful group exercise instruction, include knowing participants' health histories, being available to orient new participants before class, and having music cued and equipment ready to go before class. (b) Preparing the body for the more rigorous demands of the cardiorespiratory and/or muscular strength and conditioning segments by raising the internal temperature. (c) Improving cardiorespiratory endurance and body composition and keeping the heart rate elevated for a sustained period of time. (d) Improving muscular strength and endurance and body composition using progressive resistance. (e) Improving flexibility and concluding with relaxation/ visualization.

II. (a) A student-centered instructor establishes independence, encouragement, and attainable and realistic goals. A teacher-centered instructor fosters dependence, intimidation, unattainable goals, and quick fixes. (b) Hydrostatic weighing is more precise but not easy to access. Anthropometric assessments are not as precise but are easy to access. (c) HRmax formula does not take into account the resting heart rate. (d) High waist-to-hip ratio is associated with greater health risk for heart disease, diabetes, and some forms of cancer.

III. (a) calves, hamstrings, pectorals, hip flexors, and anterior deltoids, (b) quads, calves, and hamstrings, (c) the muscles that surround the hips

IV. (a) 3–5 days per week, (b) 55–90% of HRmax and 40–85% of $\dot{V}O_2$max, (c) 20–60 minutes or 10-minute bouts accumulated throughout the day to equal 20–60 minutes, (d) walk, run, row, stairs, cycle, and aerobics, (e) One set of 8–12 reps (f) two to four reps of a stretch for each of the major muscle groups held for 15–30 seconds each

V. (a) Place the fingertips of the first two fingers at the radial site at the wrist in line with the thumb. (b) Place the fingertips of the first two fingers to the side of the larynx. Remember to press lightly. (c) Place the first two fingers lightly on your temple.

VI. (a) (MHR = 220 - age); 220 - 45 = 175 bpm, (b) (HRR = MHR - RHR); 175 - 65 = 110 bpm, (c) 85% = (HRR x .85) + RHR; (110 x .85) + 65 = 158.5 bpm, (d) 50% = (HRR x .50) = RHR; (110 x .50) + 65 = 120 bpm.

VII. (a) S, (b) S, (c) T, (d) S, (e) T, (f) T

VIII. (1) It allows blood flow to be redistributed from internal organs to the working muscles. (2) It allows the heart muscle time to adapt to the change from a resting to a working level. (3) It allows for an increase in respiratory rate.

IX. (a) Stretching improves flexibility and therefore improves muscle performance. (b) Proper stretching requires holding the muscle, which lowers intensity, therefore defeating the purpose of the warm-up.

X. (1) Target HR formula, (2) Ratings of Perceived Exertion (RPE) scale, (3) dyspnea scale, (4) talk test

Show What You Know

I. (a) above average, (b) fitness, (c) high risk, (d) excellent, (e) poor

II. (a) 26.6; BMI = weight/(height)^2; (weight in kg = 165 lb / 2.2 = 75 kg); (height in meters = 66 inches x 2.52 cm/inch = 167.64 cm; 167.64 cm = 1.68 meters; 75/(1.68)^2 = 26.6, (b) overweight

Chapter Seven: Teaching a Group Exercise Class

Expand Your Knowledge

I. (a) 4, (b) 3, (c) 1, (d) 2

II. (a) 1. Does this particular exercise effectively stretch the muscles it is supposed to stretch? 2. Does the selected exercise cause pain in the joints or does it put unnecessary stress on the other vulnerable parts of the body? (b) 1. Does this particular exercise effectively strengthen the muscle it is supposed to strengthen? 2. Does the selected exercise cause pain in the joints or does it put unnecessary stress on the other vulnerable parts of the body? (c) 1. Does this particular exercise do what it is supposed to do? 2. Does the selected exercise cause pain in the joints or put unnecessary stress on the other vulnerable parts of the body?

III. (a) 1, (b) 4, (c) 3, (d) 5, (e) 2

IV. (a) CD, (b) AD, (c) AD, (d) MD, (e) CD, (f) MD

V. (a) enhance motivation to learn, (b) progress gradually from simple to complex, (c) offer feedback

VI. (a) 2, (b) 3, (c) 1, (d) 4

VII. (a) 120 to 140, (b) 120 to 140, (c) 120 to 160, (d) 110 to 130, (e) under 100

VIII. (a) 5, (b) 4, (c) 1, (d) 3, (e) 2, (f) 6

IX. (1) informational rather than controlling, (2) based on performance standards, (3) specific, (4) immediate

X. (a) II, (b) III, (c) IV, (d) I, (e), IV, (f) II

Show What You Know

I. (a)

1	2	3	4	5	6	7	8
four		three		arms	press	side	HUP!

(b)

1	2	3	4	5	6	7	8
four		three		toe	tap	front	clap

(c)

1	2	3	4	5	6	7	8
four		three		knee	lift	side	

Chapter Eight: Adherence and Motivation

Expand Your Knowledge

I. (a) PRO, (b) ENV (c) PRO, (d) PER, (e) ENV, (f) PER

II. (a) lack of time, boredom, (b) 30, (c) 50, (d) three 10-minute workouts

III. (a) 7, (b) 3, (c) 6, (d) 1, (e) 2, (f) 5, (g) 4

IV. (a) Set a more realistic expectation. For example, weight loss in the order of one-half pound per week. (b) Lower the intensity of the routine for a while until the over-workers can get back into their exercise comfort zone. (c) Remind participants that everyone has their own unique body shape and no amount of exercise is going to change that basic shape. (d) Prepare the participant for the break by teaching him or her how to perform an out-of-class exercise session (e.g., beach walking).

V. (1) continuing to exercise in spite of injuries or illness, (2) extreme levels of thinness, (3) problems in interpersonal relationships, (4) feelings of extreme guilt, irritability, or depression when unable to exercise

VI. (1) listen attentively and acknowledge that you understand the participant's complaint, (2) agree on a solution, (3) follow through to make any needed changes, (4) inform the participant when the issue has been resolved

VII. (a) An RPE level of 11 is within the recommended range of 11–15. An RPE level of 16 is above the recommended range. (b) Short-term goals are for each exercise session. Long-term goals are monthly. (c) Extrinsic rewards are provided by the instructor to encourage participation. Intrinsic rewards are self-provided by the participant. (d) Transient discomfort may be increased breathing, heart rate, and sweating. A more serious sign is any sudden, sharp pain that does not dissipate or a muscle pain that does not lessen after a few days.

Show What You Know

I. *Strategy:* Give regular, positive feedback. *Rationale:* It is important that the participant not feel chastised for a perceived bad habit; praise positive behaviors and provide a good example. In this way, the participant will remain in class and potentially adopt other healthy habits (e.g., giving up smoking). *Feedback:* "You have been attending class pretty regularly" or "You have made it to every class this month."

II. *Strategy:* Develop group camaraderie. *Rationale:* It is important for class participants to feel a sense of cohesiveness, or a sense of belonging. *Ice-breaker:* During the warm-up or cool-down, have each participant introduce themselves and add a "tidbit" of information about themselves (e.g., where they are from).

Chapter Nine: Disabilities and Health Limitations

Expand Your Knowledge

I. (a) A hemorrhagic stroke is caused by a ruptured blood vessel in the brain, and is more life-threatening. Ischemic strokes are caused by reduced blood supply to the brain, and are more common. (b) Hypoglycemia is a blood glucose level below 60 mg/dL and is considered more dangerous. Hyperglycemia is a high blood glucose level. (c) A participant with blood glucose lower than 100 mg/dL needs to con-

sume a rapidly absorbing carbohydrate to raise blood glucose prior to exercising. A participant with blood glucose above 300 mg/dL needs to lower blood glucose levels prior to exercising. (d) Young people who take their medication prior to exercising may be able to exercise at very high intensity levels. Older individuals may have greater difficulty exercising at moderately high (60–75% of target heart rate) intensity levels. (e) See Table 9.5 on page 257.

II. (1) Make activity as enjoyable and pain-free as possible. (2) Keep the activity at an intensity level that does not cause pain and soreness. (3) Understand the caloric balance equation. (4) Employ cross-training programs. (5) Modify equipment to make it comfortable. (6) Perform resistance training 10 to 15 minutes a day, three days a week.

III. (a) ES, (b) LS, (c) LS, (d) ES, (e) LS, (f) ES

IV. (1) rest and relax, (2) take medication, (3) drink warm liquids

V. The Americans with Disabilities Act requires that fitness centers be barrier-free so that persons with physical disabilities can participate in the same kinds of programs that are offered to nondisabled members.

VI. (a) 6 to 12 reps, (b) 1 to 3 sets, (c) 2 to 3 days per week

VII. (a) Modify the exercise to another chest exercise or to an isometric chest exercise that does not cause pain in the joint. (b) Modify activities to a seated position when possible, and to avoid accidents with weights, modify free weights to machines. (c) Modify the exercise to one that is more weight-bearing, to improve bone density. (d) It may be necessary to modify the current bike seat to make it wider and softer; it also may be necessary to raise the seat so that his or her stomach does not impair the ability to pedal the bike.

VIII. When working with a person with coronary heart disease it is important to keep the heart rate within the levels

prescribed by his or her physician to avoid another coronary event.

Show What You Know

I. (a) total-body elliptical machine: exercise machines that use all four limbs simultaneously seem to have the most benefit for persons with arthritis; also, the stair climber causes knee discomfort in many clients with arthritis, (b) wake-up workout: persons with osteoarthritis tend to perform better in the morning, (c) Swimming is one of the best activities for MS patients, provided that the water temperature is relatively cool (below 80˚); warm water will cause premature fatigue, (d) steady-state training: persons with coronary heart disease should avoid large fluctuations in heart rate

II. The student does not know what type of class would best fit his or her body type. Recommend a class more appropriate for a beginner. If no other options are available, recommend that the student come for 10 minutes at a time during the weight-training portion of the class. If the student is able to enjoy the experience, more time can be added.

Chapter Ten: Exercise and Pregnancy

Expand Your Knowledge

I. (b) X, (c) X, (e) X

II. (a) Absolute contraindication is a situation that makes exercise absolutely inadvisable. Relative contraindication is a situation in which the potential benefits associated with exercising outweigh the risks. (b) Lordotic curve is located in the lower spine, lumbar region. The kyphotic curve is located in the upper spine, thoracic region. (c) Moderately active athletes had higher birth weights. Athletes that maintain or increase their exercise late in the pregnancy had lower birth weights. (d) Fetal temperature is slightly higher than maternal temperature.

III. (1) maternal hormones, (2) mechanical stress within the abdominal cavity, (3) weak abdominal muscles

IV. (a) ↑, (b) ↑, (c)↓, (d)↑, (e)←→, (f)←→, (g)↓, (h) ←→

V. (a) backache, (b) first, (c) carpal tunnel syndrome, (d) 27, 34, (e) 6 weeks

VI. (a) position students in semirecumbent position, (b) standing may be more comfortable, (c) a towel roll may be used to support the neck and the abdominal wall; the knee and hip joints can be flexed for a more relaxed position, (d) caution participants to stretch in an average-to-normal range of motion to protect potentially hypermobile joints

VII. (1) circulatory demands of exercise and those of pregnancy; may result in decreased oxygen supply and nutrient supply, (2) carbohydrate utilization; may result in compromised fetal energy supply, (3) thermoregulation; may result in fetal hyperthermia

VIII. (a) an exaggeratedly curved lower back, rounded upper back, and a forward neck, (b) back extensors, hip flexors, shoulder protractors, shoulder internal rotators, and neck extensors, (c) abdominals, gluteals, and scapular retractors

IX. (a) 5, (b) 3, (c) 1, (d) 2, (e) 4

Show What You Know

I. The primary concern is to prevent the student from overheating. Make sure the exercise room is well ventilated and there is good cross ventilation. Also, make sure the student drinks sufficient water and adjusts the workload to maintain mild-to-moderate intensity. Later, a wider, padded seat and higher handlebars may make the bike more comfortable. Give the student opportunities for postural breaks and recommend cleated shoes rather than toe straps.

II. It is possible the student has low blood sugar, or hypoglycemia. Determine the daily food intake, and what and when she last ate. Advise the student to eat small meals throughout the day and to eat a small snack prior to coming to class. Her symptoms are not contraindications for exercise. Let her know that if the symptoms do not improve she should contact her primary physician.

III. She can begin with conservative splinting abdominal exercises, and should avoid abdominal exercises that involve spinal rotation. During the day, she can perform intermittent isometric exercises and progress to pelvic tilts. Later she can progress from pelvic stabilization exercises to head raises and partial crunches in a semi-recumbent position.

Chapter Eleven: Injury Prevention and Emergency Procedures

Expand Your Knowledge

I. (1) prevent injury by careful preparation and execution of every exercise session, (2) provide modifications for participants with injury limitations, (3) properly handle injuries that may occur during a class

II. (a) A, (b) C, (c) C, (d) A, (e) C, (f) C, (g) A

III. (a) 3, (b) 4, (c) 1, (d) 6, (e) 5, (f) 2, (g) 7

IV. (a) A rotator cuff strain is the over-stretching, overexertion, or overuse of the musculotendonus unit of one or more of the rotator cuff muscles. A rotator cuff impingement is a pinching of the rotator cuff tendon under the coracoacromial arch when the arm is abducted. (b) A sprain is an injury to a ligament. A strain is an injury to a muscle. (c) The group fitness instructor's focus is on exercise modification and injury prevention only, not injury diagnosis and treatment. The domain of healthcare providers includes injury diagnosis and treatment.

V. (1) pain, (2) swelling and discoloration, (3) loss of range of motion, (4) loss of strength, (5) loss of functional capacity

VI. (a) 6, (b) 4, (c) 2, (d) 1, (e) 7, (f) 5, (g) 3

VII. (a) Concrete floors do not absorb shock and are dangerous for a fall. (b) Participants can catch the edge of their shoes on the carpet, which can lead to an ankle sprain or other serious injury; knee injuries can occur during pivoting. (c) During lateral movements, a lack of lateral support can lead to the foot rolling over the base of support and cause an ankle sprain. (d) A lack of teaching progression and evaluations in the traditional setting can lead to poor execution and injury.

VIII. (a) 4, (b) 1, 8 , (c) 3, (d) 7, (e) 4, 5, 6, (f) 2

IX. (1) avoid motion that causes an increase in pain, (2) always engage the abdominal muscles for protection of the lumbar spine during motion, (3) emphasize the maintenance of good posture, (4) encourage stretching of the trunk and lower extremities to maintain full range of motion

Show What You Know

I. (a) Provide extra attention to new participants, including a verbal health screening, increased instructions, and increased observation. (b) Avoid very high repetitions and always strive for proper technique; avoid heavy loading of the area of concern, and allow adequate recovery time between sessions. (c) The main areas to monitor are heart-rate response to exercise and falling when moving around the pool deck.

II. (a) In the interest of client safety and proper treatment, refer them to their primary healthcare providers for medical clearance. If medical clearance is granted, encourage stretching for all motions of the wrist and light stretches of the wrist flexors prior to the class. (b) During class, avoid holding hand positions for a prolonged period of time, as this can cause irritation. (c) After class, monitor participants for an increase or return of symptoms from the activity and recommend that they ice the affected areas.

Chapter Twelve: Legal and Professional Responsibilities

Expand Your Knowledge

I. (a) The defendant is the person being sued. The plaintiff is the person filing the suit. (b) Contributory negligence means the plaintiff played some role in his or her own injury. Comparative negligence means the relative fault of both the plaintiff and defendant are measured to see who was most at fault. (c) Acts of omission include not doing something that should be done. Acts of commission include doing something that should not have been done. (d) A waiver releases the instructor and fitness center from all liability associated with the conduct of an exercise program and any resulting injuries. Informed consent is used to make the potential dangers of a program or test procedure known to the participant.

II. (1) the defendant had a duty to protect the plaintiff from injury, (2) the defendant failed to exercise the standard of care necessary to perform that duty, (3) the defendant's failure in duty was the proximate cause of the injury, (4) the damage or injury to the plaintiff did occur

III. (a) DI, (b) IM, (c) GL, (d) GL, (e) IM, (f) PL

IV. (a) advise the student that the articles pose a risk of injury, provide a safe area for the student to place her articles, (b) avoid using the exercise bands and inform your superior or club owner in writing of their condition; keep a copy of the letter for your files, (c) advise the participant that he should consult his healthcare provider prior to engaging in exercise, (d) inform your supervisor that since you have never taught Pilates, three months may not be enough time for you to learn to properly lead a safe and effective class; the class must be composed of instruction that is technically correct

V. (a) C, (b) C, (c) E, (d) E, (e) C, (f) E

VI. (a) 3, (b) 5, (c) 2, (d) 6, (e) 1, (f) 4

VII. (1) assumption of risk, (2) contributory negligence, (3) comparative negligence, (4) act of God

VIII. (b) X, (d) X

Show What You Know

I. (a) Advise her to contact her physician before exercising again and get medical clearance to continue to exercise during her pregnancy. Specifically, have her discuss with her physician how long she can continue to perform supine exercises. Guidelines by the American College of Obstetricians and Gynecologists (ACOG) state that "women should avoid exercise in the supine position after the first trimester." (b) Advise your supervisor, in writing, that you had the discussion with the participant and provide the ACOG guidelines for distribution to the other instructors. Keep a copy of the letter for your files.

II. (1) Was it the instructor's duty to provide proper instruction? Yes. (2) Was the duty satisfactorily performed? Probably not. (3) Was the instructor's failure to provide safe instruction the direct cause of the injury? It probably was. (4) Did actual damages occur? Yes, they did.